# *almost*
# Too Cute
# TO EAT

Adorable Treats,
Silly Snacks...
**Delicious Fun!**

# Make it easy - Make it fun!

Everyone will love the cute little gems you create from this book. For parties, lunchtime fun or simply to brighten a dull day, these easy-to-follow directions will have you decorating like a pro.

Most of the projects in this book are designed to save you time by using pre-packaged convenience foods, mixes and ready-to-use frostings. But you can purchase baked goods from the bakery or make them from scratch if you'd rather (there are even a few delicious from-scratch recipes at the back of the book to get you started).

Use the photos throughout the book as a decorating guide. Invite the kids to help and let your imaginations run wild!

## The kids are gonna love it!

Printed in the United States of America
by G&R Publishing Co.

Distributed By:

507 Industrial Street
Waverly, IA 50677

ISBN-13: 978-1-56383-409-7
ISBN-10: 1-56383-409-X
Item #7068

# Oatmeal Bears

Preheat oven to 375°. Line cookie sheets with parchment paper. For each bear, roll oatmeal cookie dough* into one 1¼" ball for head and three ½" balls for ears and snout, rolling one of the small balls in sugar. Place head on prepared cookie sheet; flatten slightly. Position sugared ball on lower half of head for snout. Set ears against top of head with space between. Flatten ears and snout slightly. Bake 8 to 10 minutes or until light brown. Immediately add mini M&Ms for eyes and a plain M&M for nose, pressing gently to secure. Cool on cookie sheets. Use writing icing and decorating sprinkles for bows, if desired.

\* Example uses Oatmeal Cookies recipe, page 59.

# Bow-Wow Pupcakes & Purr-dy Catty Cakes

**Makes 1 dozen of each**

## You'll Need

1 (1 lb.) tub lemon ready-to-use frosting

24 standard cupcakes*

🦴 24 rectangular cookies**

🦴 24 black, brown and/or yellow Necco wafers

36 brown plain M&Ms

🦴 Black writing gel

🐟 1 to 1½ (1.55 oz.) Hershey's Milk Chocolate candy bar

🐟 12 chocolate-flavored marshmallows

🐟 12 brown mini M&Ms

🐟 Black licorice, any type

🐟 Red Fruit Roll-Up

🦴 = Pupcakes only    🐟 = Catty Cakes only

# Directions

Set aside about 2 tablespoons frosting. Cover the tops of cupcakes evenly with remaining frosting.

**For pupcakes:** Press two cookies into frosting along opposite sides of 12 cupcakes for ears. Place two Necco wafers side by side at the top inside edges of cookies for eyes, attaching with a little set-aside frosting. Press one brown plain M&M into frosting below eyes for the nose. Using writing gel, draw the mouth and add dots on eyes and snout, if desired.

**For catty cakes:** Using a sharp knife, cut 24 small triangles from candy bar(s) for ears. Place two triangles in frosting near the top of 12 cupcakes. Press two yellow plain M&Ms into frosting below ears for eyes. Place one brown mini M&M centered below eyes for the nose. Slice the ends off 12 chocolate marshmallows and press them side by side into frosting under nose, uncut side up (the middles make a great snack while you're decorating). Cut licorice into short, thin pieces and insert three pieces into frosting on each side of marshmallows for whiskers. Cut tongue shapes from Fruit Roll-Up and insert into frosting under marshmallows. Using writing gel, draw vertical lines on eyes.

\* Example uses lemon cake mix to match these lively personalities.

\*\* Example uses Mother's brand Coconut Cocadas.

**Plan ahead**

Candles need to set overnight.

# Quickie Cookie Cakes

Makes 1 dozen cakes

## You'll Need

- 3 Tootsie Fruit Rolls, any color
- 1 vanilla-flavored Tootsie Fruit Roll
- 24 cream-filled vanilla cookies
- 8 cubes white almond bark (about 13 oz.)
- Decorating sprinkles
- ¼ C. white decorating icing
- Paste food coloring, any color
- Small zippered plastic bag
- 12 paper cupcake liners, optional

# Directions

Unwrap Tootsies and press each into a flattened square. Cut each colored square into four equal pieces. Cut vanilla square into 12 tiny slices. Wrap a colored square around a vanilla slice, sealing ends together to create 12 "candles" (candles that are slightly thicker are more durable). Cut a thin slice from the bottom of each candle, if necessary, so bottom is flat. Let set overnight to harden.

Remove any crumbs from cookies. Melt almond bark according to package directions. Attach flat sides of two cookies together with a dab of melted bark to make a double layer "cake"; set aside to harden. Reheat bark if necessary and use it to "frost" top and sides of one cake. Set cake on waxed paper. Place a candy candle on top and hold in place until it stands upright on cake. Decorate top of cake with sprinkles while bark is still wet. Repeat with remaining cakes. Let dry.

In a small bowl, tint icing with food coloring until desired shade is reached. Transfer icing to plastic bag and cut a tiny corner from bag. Pipe icing around top edge of cakes. Set each cake in a cupcake liner, if desired. Serve immediately.

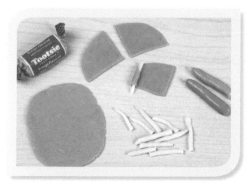

# Runaway Picnic Ants

Makes 1 dozen ants

## You'll Need

1 C. white ready-to-use frosting, divided

Brown paste food coloring

Pastry bag fitted with a small writing tip

¾ C. sweetened flaked coconut

Green paste food coloring

12 (3½″) sugar cookies

36 chocolate-covered peanuts

Black paste food coloring

12 red gourmet fruit slice candies

1 cube chocolate almond bark (about 1.6 oz.)

Small zippered plastic bag

# *Directions*

In a small bowl, tint ¼ cup frosting with brown food coloring until desired shade is reached. Transfer brown frosting to pastry bag. Tint coconut with green food coloring;* set aside.

Place remaining ¾ cup frosting in a separate small bowl; tint with green food coloring until desired shade is reached. Cover the top of cookies evenly with green frosting, using about 1 tablespoon for each cookie. Place three chocolate-covered peanuts end-to-end down the middle of each cookie to form ants' bodies. Sprinkle tinted coconut on frosting around ant.

Dip a toothpick into black food coloring to make two small eyes on ants and tiny dots on fruit slice candies to resemble watermelon seeds. Melt almond bark according to package directions. Use melted bark to attach one fruit slice to the top of each ant, holding in place a few seconds to secure.

Using brown frosting, pipe legs and antennae on each ant.

*\* To tint, place coconut in a small zippered plastic bag and add a small amount of food coloring. Rub coconut and coloring together inside bag until coconut is tinted to desired color.*

# Birds of a Feather

## Makes 2 dozen nests

## You'll Need

1 (11 oz.) pkg. butterscotch chips

¾ C. crunchy peanut butter

5 to 6 C. chow mein noodles

Blue and pink Mike & Ike candies*

Blue and pink malted milk ball eggs

Yellow writing icing

Black paste food coloring

Candy-coated almonds**

# Directions

Line a work surface with waxed paper. Melt butterscotch chips according to package directions. Stir in peanut butter until well blended. Stir in chow mein noodles until noodles are well coated. Use mixture to create nests about 3″ in diameter and 1¼″ high; set on waxed paper to dry.

Cut Mike & Ikes in half crosswise and press cut side of each half onto each side of a malted milk ball egg for wings. Create a bird's beak on the front of egg with a drop of writing icing. Dip a toothpick into food coloring and make two small dots for eyes. Let dry.

Place one or two birds in each nest with candy-coated almonds as desired.

Sweet TWEETS!

\* Example uses Berry Blast Mike & Ikes.

\*\* Example uses pastel-colored Jordan almonds.

# Cell Phone Fun

Makes 5 cell phones

## You'll Need

1¼ C. white ready-to-use frosting

Paste food coloring, any color

10 graham cracker rectangles

5 rolls Sweet Tart or Smarties candies

1 Fruit Roll-Up, any flavor

Edible food marker

# Directions

In a small bowl, tint frosting with food coloring until desired shade is reached. Sandwich two crackers together with a thin layer of frosting. Repeat for all crackers.

Cover each top cracker with a smooth layer of frosting. Working from the bottom up, place candies in five rows of three for phone buttons, pressing lightly into frosting to adhere.

Unroll Fruit Roll-Up and cut into five 1½ x 2″ pieces for cell phone "screens"; press in place, centered above candies. Let dry several minutes.

With food marker, write numerals and symbols (left and right arrows, OK, * and #) on candy buttons. Print a text message* on the screen, if desired. Let dry.

* Write a simple abbreviation or print

a fun message like "PLS come 2 my PRTY!"

**Plan ahead**

Large fondant pieces need to dry about 48 hours before using.

# Just Another Face in the Crowd

# You'll Need

Powdered sugar for dusting

Fondant*

4½" lollipop sticks, optional

1 (1 lb.) tub white ready-to-use frosting

Paste food coloring in various colors

24 standard cupcakes**

# Directions

Dust work surface with powdered sugar. Roll small pieces of fondant into ropes to help shape features like arms, ears and horns. Roll dough into balls for eyes and warts. To make eyes extend above cupcakes, insert a lollipop stick into the bottom of each eye while dough is still soft. Place all shapes on waxed paper to dry. To help retain their shape, let larger pieces dry about 48 hours.

To cut out flat objects such as mouths, tongues and teeth, roll dough to 1/16" thickness. Cut into desired shapes using

*recipe continued on next page*

cookie cutters, a knife or kitchen shears. To attach one dough piece to another, use a bit of water.

Set aside a small amount of frosting to pipe on additional features or decorations, if desired. In a small bowl, tint remaining frosting with food coloring as desired and cover the tops of cupcakes with frosting. Decorate freshly frosted cupcakes as desired using dried fondant pieces. Attach larger fondant pieces such as arms and horns by carefully inserting them through frosting and partway into cupcakes; smaller pieces can be attached by setting directly onto wet frosting.

For best results, serve cupcakes the same day the fondant pieces are added.

* Example uses Marshmallow Fondant recipe, pages 60 and 61.

Or purchase ready-to-use fondant where cake decorating supplies are sold.

** Example uses orange-flavored cupcakes for a monstrously colorful treat!

# Antler Brigade

Break any type of pretzels into pieces that resemble antlers. Remove any crumbs from 10 Nutter Butter cookies. Melt about 20 peanut butter candy wafers according to package directions. Cover the top of one cookie with a smooth layer of melted candy coating. Immediately add plain M&Ms for the nose and the ears, if desired. Add mini M&Ms for the eyes. Attach pretzel pieces while coating is still wet; hold in place or prop them up until set. When coating is dry, add a dot of white writing icing to the eyes and use red writing icing to create a mouth, if desired.

# I'm No Dum-Dum Mini Cupcakes

**Makes 36 cupcakes**

## You'll Need

1 (1 lb.) tub white or chocolate ready-to-use frosting

Green paste food coloring, optional

36 mini cupcakes*

Green nonpareils, optional

36 Dum Dum pops, any color

Mike and Ike candies, any color

Green Tootsie Fruit Rolls, optional

# Directions

In a small bowl, tint white frosting with green food coloring, if desired, until desired shade is reached. Cover the top of each cupcake with white, green or chocolate frosting. Sprinkle with nonpareils, if desired.

Unwrap Dum Dum pops. Use kitchen shears to cut off about 1″ from the stick of each pop. Cut four Mike and Ikes in half crosswise and press the cut edge of each half against the rim of one pop for flower petals, covering the rim. Repeat for each pop. Unwrap Tootsies and press to flatten, softening in microwave a few seconds if needed. Use kitchen shears to cut leaf shapes from Tootsies, if desired.

Push the stick of one flower into each cupcake. Press one or two leaves into frosting beside flower, if desired.

\* Example uses chocolate cupcakes for a treat with an "earthy" look.

19

# Sugar Wafer Garden Boxes

Makes 7 garden boxes

## You'll Need

1 (11 oz.) pkg. cream-filled vanilla sugar wafers (3½" long)

2½ T. chocolate frosting

1 cube white almond bark (about 1.6 oz.)

Small zippered plastic bag

Orange and green paste food coloring (carrots only)

Paste food coloring, various colors (flowers only)

Marzipan*

Green jelly beans (flowers only)

# Directions

Crush eight wafers. Transfer to a small bowl and add frosting; stir to blend well. Set aside to use for "dirt".

For each garden box, you will need four cookies; one for the bottom of the box and three for the sides (cut one of the three cookies in half crosswise). Melt almond bark according to package directions; cool about 1 minute. Transfer melted bark to plastic bag and cut a tiny corner from bag. Pipe a small bead of bark along two long sides of one cookie (bottom of the box). Attach one uncut cookie upright onto bark on each side; press to adhere. Pipe bark along short ends of bottom cookie; attach half cookies upright, pressing to adhere. Repeat for each box. Divide set-aside dirt mixture evenly among boxes. Use the end of a wooden spoon handle to make three evenly spaced holes in the dirt.

**For carrots:** Tint a small ball of marzipan orange. Roll dough into carrot shapes. Tint a small ball of marzipan green and make teardrop shapes for stems; flatten slightly. Press the pointed end of each stem onto rounded end of each carrot. Use kitchen shears to snip the end of the stem two or three times. Bury carrots partway into holes in dirt.

**For flowers:** Tint small balls of marzipan with food coloring for flower petals and contrasting flower centers. Shape five petals for each flower; press together, overlapping in the middle. Shape flower centers and push gently onto flowers. Attach a jelly bean "stem" to the bottom of each flower, pressing gently to adhere. Bury jelly beans partway into holes in dirt.

*Example uses Marzipan recipe, pages 62 and 63.

# Not-So-Scary Scarecrow Cookies

**Makes 1 dozen scarecrows**

## You'll Need

1 C. cream cheese ready-to-use frosting, divided

Paste food coloring, any color

Small zippered plastic bag

12 (3″ to 3½″) round sugar cookies

18 (3½″) cream-filled sugar wafers, any color

Gumdrops, optional

24 Skittles, any color

12 jelly beans, any color

Tinted or toasted coconut*

Licorice, chuckles or fruit slice candies, cut into thin pieces

# Directions

In a small bowl, tint ¼ cup frosting with food coloring until desired shade is reached for hat trim; transfer to plastic bag and cut a tiny corner from bag. Set aside.

Cover the tops of cookies evenly with untinted frosting.

Using a sharp knife, cut six sugar wafers in half crosswise. Place one wafer half at the top edge of each frosted cookie; press to adhere. Place an uncut wafer just below the half wafer, creating a hat. Pipe a thin line of frosting from bag where the two wafers meet. Attach a gumdrop to the hat, if desired.

Add Skittles for eyes and a jelly bean for a nose. Attach a small piece of licorice, curved upward, for a mouth. Press coconut into frosting for hair. Use any remaining frosting in bag to pipe on dots in the center of eyes, eye lashes, decorative details on hats and other features, if desired.

*To tint, place coconut in a small zippered plastic bag and add a small amount of yellow food coloring. Rub coconut and coloring together inside bag until coconut is tinted to desired color. To toast instead, place coconut in a single layer in a dry skillet over medium heat or on a baking sheet in a 350° oven for 5 to 8 minutes or until golden brown.*

# Wise Guys with Puffy Eyes

Makes 1 dozen owls

## You'll Need

12 chocolate graham cracker squares

12 regular marshmallows

24 pieces candy corn

12 half-dollar size chocolate coins, optional

30 yellow candy wafers, divided

24 brown plain M&Ms

1½ (1.55 oz.) Hershey's Milk Chocolate candy bars, divided

Hoooo...

# Directions

Preheat oven to 250°. Arrange graham crackers about 1½˝ apart on a baking sheet. Cut marshmallows in half crosswise and place two halves, cut side down, near the top of each cracker for eyes. Tuck one piece of candy corn, pointed side down, between inside edges of marshmallows for beak. Bake about 7 minutes or until marshmallows are soft and slightly puffy.

To make owls with chocolate coin eyes, unwrap coins and cut in half. Place one coin half near the top of each warm marshmallow, rounded side toward the top, pressing down lightly to adhere to marshmallow. Melt six candy wafers as directed on package. Use melted candy coating to attach one full yellow wafer, flat side up, to each coin half. Attach one M&M to each yellow wafer to complete the eyes. If not using coins, simply press round candy wafers, flat side up, directly into warm marshmallows. Then use melted candy coating to attach M&Ms to yellow wafers to complete the eyes.

Break candy bars along score lines to make 12 rectangles; cut rectangles in half diagonally to form 24 triangle ears. Tuck the wide end of each ear behind a cooled marshmallow.

For best results, serve owls immediately.

**Or try this:** Use green and yellow candy wafers and blue plain M&Ms for eyes, an orange gourmet fruit slice candy for a beak and various colors gourmet fruit slice candies for feathers, placing all pieces into warm marshmallows.

# Candy Shanties

Makes 2 dozen shanties

## You'll Need

5 T. butter

1 (10.5 oz.) bag mini marshmallows

9 C. crisp rice cereal

7 to 8 cubes white almond bark (about 11 to 12 oz.)

Assorted candies, pretzels, cookies and decorating sprinkles and pearls*

# Directions

Line a 9 x 13″ pan with aluminum foil, extending foil over edges of pan. Lightly spray foil with nonstick cooking spray; set aside. In a large saucepan over medium heat, melt butter and marshmallows, stirring constantly until mixture is smooth. Remove from heat and add cereal; stir to coat. Transfer mixture to prepared pan; press evenly with buttered hands; set aside to cool completely. Use ends of foil to remove cooled cereal mixture from pan. Trim away ½″ from each side of mixture (yummy to eat while you're decorating shanties). Cut into 24 (2″) squares. Cut 12 squares in half diagonally. Press sets of two triangles together, matching points to create roofs.

Melt almond bark according to package directions. Dip the top of one square into melted bark and set on waxed paper. Press one roof onto wet bark. Continue with remaining squares and roofs.

Use remaining melted bark to attach Sour Punch Straws or chocolate rock candies to the front of the shanties for siding, or simply "paint" with melted bark. Attach Fruit by the Foot, sliced Chuckles or Kit Kat pieces for doors. Try using Petite Mints, jumbo flower sprinkles or rectangular pretzels for shingles. Chimneys can be made from items like gumdrops or stacked chocolate rock candies. Accessorize by attaching decorating pearls for doorknobs and trim, candy cane pieces for archways or gourmet fruit slice candies for windows.

# Prefab Gift Box Treats

Makes 10 gift boxes

Unwrap fancy frosted white snack cakes from a 10-count package. Unwrap Fruit Roll-Ups and use kitchen shears or a pizza cutter to cut strips long enough to wrap around the top and sides of each cake to resemble ribbons, pressing lightly to adhere to frosting. Dip bottom of cakes in powdered sugar before setting on work surface to prevent roll-ups from sticking. Decorate top of cakes with additional strips of roll-ups, decorating sprinkles and small candies, attaching with a bit of icing or melted almond bark, as desired. Pick up cakes by undecorated areas only. For best results serve the same day they're decorated.

# Bundled up Snowmen

Makes 10 snowmen

Remove any crumbs from 10 Nutter Butter cookies. Melt four cubes white almond bark (about 6.4 ounces) according to package directions. Place a cookie in melted bark and lift with a fork. Using a spoon, pour additional bark over the top and sides of cookie to coat; tap fork gently against bowl to remove excess bark. Lay coated cookie on waxed paper. While coating is wet, add decorating sprinkles and nonpareils for buttons and facial features. Repeat with remaining cookies. When cookies dry, cut thin strips from Fruit by the Foot or Fruit Roll-Ups for scarves; loop around cookies as desired. For each hat, cut a 3˝ rectangle from Fruit by the Foot. Wrap around the cookie, overlapping in back; push gently to adhere. Cut strips for headbands and attach the same way.

# Frogs in Candyland

Makes 2 dozen frogs

## You'll Need

Royal Icing*

Green paste food coloring

24 standard cupcakes**

1 cube chocolate almond bark (about 1.6 oz.)

48 brown mini M&Ms

48 green gourmet fruit slice candies or large green gumdrops***

Green mini M&Ms

Red Fruit by the Foot

Red writing icing

# Directions

In a small bowl, tint icing with food coloring until desired shade is reached. Cover the top of cupcakes evenly with green icing.

Melt almond bark according to package directions. Attach an M&M to each fruit slice with a tiny dab of melted bark to complete the eyes. Place eyes in wet icing near back edge of cupcakes, flat edge down. Set green M&Ms in frosting for nostrils.

Using a sharp knife, cut a slit near the front of each cupcake just above paper liner, about ⅜″ wide and ½″ deep. Unroll Fruit by the Foot and cut 24 strips about ⅜″ wide and 3″ to 4″ long. Insert one end of fruit strip into each slit for a tongue. Use writing icing to draw a mouth above the tongue.

\* Example uses Royal Icing recipe, page 57.

\*\* Example uses Pistachio Cupcakes recipe, page 56.

\*\*\* If gumdrops are used, slice in half from the top down and attach an M&M to cut side.

# Lambs from the Land of Milan

Makes 8 lambs

## You'll Need

10 C. popped popcorn

1 C. sugar

½ C. light corn syrup

¼ C. butter

Pinch of salt

½ tsp. clear vanilla extract

1 cube chocolate almond bark (about 1.6 oz.)

8 Milano cookies

16 mini marshmallows

1 cube white almond bark (about 1.6 oz.)

16 mini chocolate chips

32 chocolate-covered peanuts

# Directions

Pour popcorn into a large bowl; set aside.

In a medium saucepan over medium heat, combine sugar, corn syrup, butter, salt and 2 tablespoons water. Stir and heat to about 275° (soft-crack stage). Remove from heat and stir in vanilla; mix well. Pour mixture evenly over popcorn in bowl and stir to coat all pieces. Let cool 2 to 3 minutes. Butter hands and shape mixture into eight 3″ to 4″ balls. Place on waxed paper to cool.

Melt chocolate almond bark according to package directions. Cover one flat side of each cookie with melted bark; let dry. Cut mini marshmallows in half crosswise. Melt white almond bark according to package directions. Use a dab of melted white bark to attach a chocolate chip to the uncut side of half the marshmallows for eyes. Gently squeeze the remaining marshmallow halves to resemble ears. Use melted white bark to attach ears and eyes to chocolate side of cookies.

Using a sharp knife, slice a small area off each popcorn ball where the lamb's face will be. Attach face to popcorn ball using melted white almond bark; hold in place briefly. Use melted bark to attach four chocolate-covered peanuts under each lamb for feet.* Let set until dry.

*Try dipping rounded side of four chocolate-covered peanuts in melted white almond bark and placing on a work surface in a small square. Set popcorn ball on top of peanuts, pushing gently to adhere. It may be necessary to cut a bit of popcorn from bottom of lambs to create a flat surface for feet.*

# Funky Little Party Hats

Makes 1 dozen hats

## You'll Need

2 (10-count) boxes Fruit
Roll-Ups in various colors

1 (12-count) box sugar
cones

1 cube white almond
bark (about 1.6 oz.)

Small zippered plastic bag

12 (2″) round or scalloped-
edge cookies*

M&Ms, popcorn, mini
marshmallows or
other small treats

# Directions

Unwrap Fruit Roll-Ups, a few at a time. Using kitchen shears, small cookie cutters or a pizza cutter, cut strips, triangles or other shapes from roll-ups. Apply shapes to outside of cones, overlapping if desired and pressing to adhere.

Melt almond bark according to package directions; let cool about 1 minute. Transfer melted bark to plastic bag and cut a tiny corner from bag. Tip a decorated cone rim side up and fill with treats. Pipe a small bead of bark onto rim of cone. Keeping cone rim side up, place a cookie on wet bark to cover open end of cone and press to seal. Tip cone pointed end up and let dry.

Add tassels to hats using short strips of roll-ups, as desired.

\* Or large enough to completely cover the opening in cones.

**Plan ahead**

Royal Icing needs to dry several hours or overnight.

# Postcard Pastries

Makes 8 postcards

Unwrap pastries from an 8-count package of any flavor Pop-Tarts. Place Pop-Tarts, unfrosted side up, on a work surface. Tint Royal Icing* with paste food coloring as desired and use it to cover unfrosted side of Pop-Tarts. Let dry several hours or until icing is completely dry to the touch. Use edible food markers or writing icing for lettering and decorate edges of postcards with writing icing and/or heart-shaped sprinkles. Create postage stamps with writing icing, heart-shaped candies or Starburst candies cut in half horizontally.

* Example uses Royal Icing recipe, page 57.

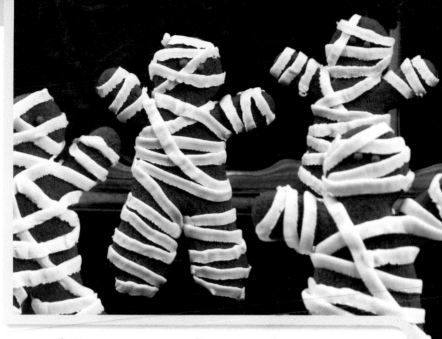

# Mummified Gingers

**Makes 18 mummies**

Use writing icing to make small round eyes on gingerbread cookies.* Transfer about half of a 1-pound tub white ready-to-use frosting to a pastry bag fitted with a small flat tip. Pipe frosting back and forth across and over the sides of cookies to resemble bandages. Add more frosting to bag as necessary to finish cookies.

\* Example uses Gingerbread Cookies recipe, page 58.

# Barnyard Parade

# You'll Need

Paste food coloring (pink, yellow, black, red and orange)

Fondant*

Powdered sugar for dusting

1˝ round cookie cutter

18 round cream-filled vanilla cookies

20 pink candy wafers (pig only)

20 yellow candy wafers (duck only)

80 white candy wafers (sheep, cows, bunnies and roosters)

Mini marshmallows (sheep only)

White writing icing

# Directions

Add food coloring to small balls of fondant dough (about 1½˝ in diameter), making one ball of each color and matching yellow and pink colors to yellow and pink candy wafers.

Dust work surface with powdered sugar. Roll dough, one color at a time, to ⅛˝ thickness. Cut faces for each animal using cookie cutter. Use a knife or toothpick to cut out features such as roosters' combs. Roll bits of dough into tiny ropes for features such as cows' horns and pigs' and cows' tails. Roll dough into tiny "logs" for pigs' legs.  Shape dough into small balls to make hooves for sheep and cows and noses for bunnies; flatten balls for features such as cows' spots and noses for sheep and pigs. Shape dough into ears, beaks and wattles. Set all shapes on waxed paper to dry.

Remove any crumbs from cookies. Melt candy wafers, one color at a time, according to package directions. You will

*recipe continued on next page*

# Directions cont.

need to cover three cookies with melted pink coating, three with yellow coating and 12 with white coating. Place a cookie in the melted coating. Lift cookie with a fork. Using a spoon, pour additional candy coating over the top and sides of cookie to coat; tap fork gently against bowl to remove excess coating. Lay coated cookie on waxed paper to dry. Repeat with additional cookies.

If coating in bowl has dried, simply reheat and use a small dab to attach faces, marshmallows and features to coated cookies. When fondant is being attached directly to fondant, a bit of water can be used instead of melted coating, if desired. Attach bunny faces near the bottom of cookies; all other faces can be centered. Cut marshmallows in half crosswise and attach around face of sheep, cut side down. Attach remaining features as shown in photo. Some features such as smaller eyes on pigs, ducks and roosters can be created using writing icing and/or a toothpick dipped in black food coloring.

* Example uses Marshmallow Fondant recipe, pages 60 and 61.

Or purchase ready-to-use fondant where cake decorating supplies are sold.

40

# *House Mouse Meets Laughing Cow*

Makes 16 mice

Unwrap wedges from a 6-ounce wheel of Laughing Cow cheese (any flavor); cut each in half horizontally, creating 16 equal wedges. Place each on a snack cracker that is at least the size of the cheese wedge. Cut 16 thin strips from a green onion top, curl each around a straw and place curls in ice water. Use the end of the straw to cut 16 round pieces from black olives; attach one to the pointed end of each wedge for the nose. Attach caraway seeds for eyes. Cut 32 thin slices from small carrots and press into the top of wedges for ears. Remove onions from water; drain briefly on a paper towel. Insert one end of each onion curl into the rounded end of each wedge for a tail. Serve immediately.

# Pretty Little Mallow Cakes

Makes 2 dozen flowers

## You'll Need

1 (1 lb.) tub white ready-to-use frosting

24 standard cupcakes*

24 to 30 regular marshmallows

Colored decorating sugar

24 mini Sweet Tarts or plain M&Ms

# Directions

Set aside about 1 tablespoon frosting. Cover the top of cupcakes evenly with remaining frosting.

Spray blades of kitchen shears with nonstick cooking spray and cut marshmallows crosswise into four or five even slices. Immediately sprinkle colored sugar on one cut side of each slice. Arrange five slices in a circle on top of each cupcake, overlapping "petals" and keeping center points close together to form a flower. Place one piece of candy in the center of each flower, attaching with a dab of frosting.

For best results, serve cupcakes shortly after marshmallows are added.

* Example uses white cake mix for simplicity, allowing the flowers to take center stage.

# Hi-Ho & Ho-Ho-Ho

**Makes 6 Gnomes or Santas**

## You'll Need

About ½ C. candy wafers (red for Santas; any other color for Gnomes)

6 sugar cones

12 pink candy wafers

Food-safe paintbrush

Black paste food coloring

2 cubes white almond bark (about 3.2 oz.)

Zippered plastic bag

 6 red round sprinkles

6 pink heart sprinkles

6 small red gumdrops

6 red stick sprinkles

6 mini marshmallows

6 small foil-wrapped chocolate candies*

  = Santas only ▲ = Gnomes only

# Directions

### For both Gnomes and Santas: In a small bowl,
melt ½ cup candy wafers according to package directions.
Brush coating onto each cone using a food-safe paintbrush.
Set pointed end up on waxed paper to dry. Melt pink candy
wafers according to package directions. Use paintbrush to
brush a thick layer of coating onto center front of cones
to make faces. Let dry. Dip a toothpick into black food
coloring to make eyes. Melt almond bark; cool about 1
minute. Transfer melted bark to a plastic bag and cut a tiny
corner from bag.

### For Gnomes: Pipe beard on lower part and sides of face
using short straight lines, making several overlapping layers
and letting lines dry slightly between coats. Let dry. Cut off
a small slice from flat end of a gumdrop for nose and attach
with melted coating. Attach a stick sprinkle for mouth.

### For Santas: Pipe beard on lower part and sides of face
using swirled lines, making several overlapping layers and
letting lines dry slightly between coats. Pipe on a mustache
and trim for hat. Let dry. Use a drop of melted coating to
attach a round sprinkle nose and heart sprinkle mouth.
Attach a marshmallow to point of hat.

Set a foil-wrapped chocolate candy under each Santa or
Gnome for a fun surprise.

* Mini chocolate Santas or chocolate coins are options.

Make sure candies fit inside sugar cones.

# Spin Art Cookies

Makes about 9 cookies

## You'll Need

1 (1 lb. 1.5 oz.) pkg. sugar cookie mix

Butter and egg as directed on cookie mix

Paste food coloring as desired

Flour for rolling

3˝ round cookie cutter

9 (6˝) cookie sticks

Royal Icing*

Pastry bags fitted with small round tips

# *Directions*

Preheat oven to 350°. Line cookie sheet with parchment paper; set aside.

Stir together cookie mix, butter and egg as directed on package. Work in food coloring for colored dough, if desired. On a floured surface roll dough to ⅜″ thickness. Cut with cookie cutter and transfer to prepared cookie sheet, leaving room for sticks. Carefully insert stick halfway into one edge of each cookie. Bake 15 to 18 minutes or until set. Immediately transfer to a cooling rack.

Divide royal icing evenly between several small bowls. Tint all but one bowl with food coloring until desired shade is reached. Transfer colored icing to pastry bags. Cover the top of one cooled cookie with white icing. Immediately use colored icing to pipe four straight intersecting lines from one side of the cookie to the other. Pipe a second colored icing between first lines. Starting at the center of cookie, drag the tip of a toothpick through frosting in increasingly larger spirals to the edge. Repeat with remaining cookies. Let dry.

For spiral cookies, frost with colored icing; let dry. Use a pastry bag fitted with a medium round tip to pipe contrasting icing in a spiral. Sprinkle with colored sugar. Brush off excess sugar.

* Example uses Royal Icing recipe, page 57.

47

# Cupcakes with a Sunny Disposition

Makes 36 cupcakes

## You'll Need

36 mini cupcakes*

1 (1 lb.) tub chocolate ready-to-use frosting

Yellow and/or orange plain M&Ms

Chocolate decorating sprinkles

Green Chuckles candies, optional

# Directions

Cover the top of a cupcake evenly with frosting. Place 10 to 15 M&Ms around the edge of cupcake, overlapping if desired. Hold in place briefly to secure. Cover the center frosted area with chocolate sprinkles. Repeat for remaining cupcakes.

Cut Chuckles into leaf shapes to serve with cupcakes, if desired.

**Or Try This:** Make other types of flowers on frosted mini cupcakes by attaching pastel candy corn, jelly beans or candy-coated almonds for petals and mini Sweet Tarts, M&Ms or Red Hot candies for centers.

\* Example uses chocolate cupcakes to resemble chocolatey brown sunflower seeds.

# Playful Polar Penguin Pals

Makes 10 penguins

## You'll Need

10 Double Stuff Oreo cookies*

2 cubes white almond bark (about 3.2 oz.)

2 small zippered plastic bags

20 small round chocolate candy sprinkles or mini chocolate chips

2 T. white ready-to-use frosting

Orange paste food coloring

# Directions

Remove any crumbs from cookies. Set cookies on edge to determine which side should be the bottom of each penguin if you want to display them standing upright. Lay cookies flat on waxed paper. If wings will be added, separate several additional cookies and remove filling; using a sharp knife, cut narrow slices from edges. Cut each slice in half to make two small wing shapes.

Melt almond bark according to package directions; let cool about 1 minute. Transfer melted bark to a plastic bag and cut a tiny corner from bag. Pipe a small bead of bark onto cookie to outline white area; fill in with more bark and tap cookie gently on counter to smooth. Attach two candy sprinkles on wet bark for eyes. Attach wide end of wings to wet bark. Set aside to dry.

In a small bowl, tint frosting with food coloring until desired shade is reached. Transfer frosting to a separate plastic bag and cut a tiny corner from bag. On each penguin, pipe a small triangular nose and two feet. When dry, stand penguins up on edge, if desired.

* You'll need several extra cookies if you're adding wings.

# Quick Lunch Box Cuties

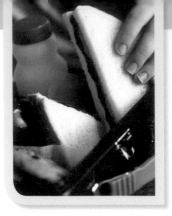

## Unforgettable Umbrellas

Cut a rounded apple in half from top to bottom through the core. Cut away a thin even slice from cut side of apple halves to remove core and seeds. Cut away a ½" (or smaller) slice from bottom of apple halves. In bottom cut side of each half, make a starter hole for the end of a straw to fit into, but do not insert straw. Lightly score vertical stripes in apple peel and remove peel from alternating stripes. Brush all cut surfaces with lemon juice. Trim both ends of two bendable straws to form the umbrella handles; insert longer end into starter holes. Each apple makes two umbrellas.

## Peeking Produce

For strawberries, wash and dry fruit. Attach eyes with a bit of melted white almond bark or cream cheese. For celery, cut stalk into pieces; wash and dry. Fill celery pieces with squeeze cheese or peanut butter. Attach candy eyeballs to cheese or peanut butter.

Cut a piece of cheese to fit on a rectangular cracker and cut small pieces for collars as desired. Cut pieces from another type of cheese for ties. Use the end of a straw to cut buttons from a black olive. Attach pieces with butter, cream cheese or squeeze cheese.

## Sassy Sammies

Build fish on a plate. Attach a slice of cheese to bread using butter, mustard, mayo or squeeze cheese. Layer a hard-cooked egg slice and black olive slice for eye. Add a black olive piece for mouth. Cut a 3″ piece from a stalk of celery and make several 2″ slits in one end; place in a bowl of ice water. Cut diagonal slices from the remainder of the stalk and arrange on cheese for scales. Add celery leaves for fins. Drain celery frill and set on plate behind fish.

## Simple Sandwiches

Build butterflies and ghosts using butter, mustard, mayo or squeeze cheese to attach the pieces. Using a cookie cutter, cut a butterfly or ghost shape from bread; cut a matching shape from a slice of cheese and attach to bread. **For butterflies**, peel a carrot, cutting a thin stick for butterfly's body and cutting several thin round slices from remainder of carrot for wing decorations. Put a bit of squeeze cheese on one end of two chow mein noodles and poke cheese ends into bread for antennae. **For ghosts**, attach mini chocolate chips for the eyes and a brown plain M&M for the mouth.

## Petite Pumpkins

Spread a layer of flavored cream cheese over one side of a 10″ sundried tomato-flavored flour tortilla. Use a pizza cutter to cut tortilla into 1″ wide strips. Place two or three strips on top of each other. Starting with a short end, roll strips together to create a spiral. Place seam side down. Repeat with remaining strips. Break a pretzel stick in thirds or use a cashew and poke into top of spiral for a stem. Poke a celery or parsley leaf into top of spiral along with the stem, if desired. Each tortilla makes three or four pumpkins.

## Krispie Kritters

Make a batch of Cocoa Krispie Treats according to recipe on cereal box. Cut into 1¾″ squares; remove from pan. Melt 1 cube chocolate almond bark (about 1.6 ounces); use for attaching pieces. **For spider**, cut four long lengths of Pull 'n' Peel licorice for legs; attach to center of a krispie square, overlapping in center. To a small peppermint patty, attach candy eyes; using writing icing, draw a mouth and fangs. Attach to center of legs. **For bird**, to a small peppermint patty, attach candy eyes and a heart-shaped sprinkle for beak. Attach to center of a krispie square. Cut another peppermint patty in fourths; attach two pieces for wings.

## Spiders and Sunshine

Sandwich two round butter crackers together with peanut butter. Break pretzel sticks in half. **For spiders**, insert broken end of four pretzel halves into peanut butter on each side of cracker for legs. Melt a couple of peanut butter candy wafers according to package directions and spread on top cracker. Attach two candy eyes. **For sunshine**, insert broken end of 15 or 16 pretzel halves into peanut butter all the way around cracker. Melt a couple of yellow candy wafers and spread on top cracker. Attach two candy eyes. When dry, pipe on a thin smile, using melted chocolate wafers or writing gel.

55

# Pistachio Cupcakes

## You'll Need

1 (18.25 oz.) pkg. vanilla cake mix

4 eggs

½ C. vegetable oil

1 (3.4 oz.) pkg. pistachio instant pudding mix

½ C. sour cream

Green paste food coloring, optional

## Directions

Preheat oven to 350°. Line standard muffin pans with paper liners. In a large mixing bowl, combine cake mix, eggs, oil, pudding mix, sour cream and ½ cup water. Beat on medium speed for 2 minutes. Slowly blend in food coloring until desired shade is reached. Transfer about 2 tablespoons batter into each cupcake liner. Bake 15 to 18 minutes or until a toothpick inserted in center comes out nearly clean. Cool.

Used for Frogs in Candyland, pages 30 and 31.

# Royal Icing

## You'll Need

3 T. meringue powder

4 C. sifted powdered sugar

Paste food coloring
as instructed in project

## Directions

In a medium mixing bowl, beat together meringue powder, powdered sugar and 6 tablespoons warm water on medium-high speed 7 to 10 minutes or until icing is smooth and soft peaks form. Stir in food coloring.

Used for Frogs in Candyland, pages 30 and 31,

Postcard Pastries, page 36

and Spin Art Cookies, pages 46 and 47.

# Gingerbread Cookies

## You'll Need

½ C. butter, softened

½ C. sugar

¼ C. molasses

1 egg

2 C. flour, plus more
for dusting

½ tsp. salt

½ tsp. baking powder

½ tsp. baking soda

½ tsp. ground cinnamon

½ tsp. ground nutmeg

1 tsp. ground cloves

1 tsp. ground ginger

1 (4˝ to 5˝) person-shaped
cookie cutter

## Directions

In a large bowl, mix butter and sugar on medium speed
until smooth. Mix in molasses and egg. In a small bowl, stir
together flour, salt, baking powder, baking soda, cinnamon,
nutmeg, cloves and ginger. Slowly add to butter mixture,
beating until well blended. Cover and chill for several hours.
Preheat oven to 350°. Dust work surface with flour. Roll
dough to ¼˝ thickness and cut with cookie cutter. Place
cookies 2˝ apart on ungreased cookie sheets. Bake
8 to 10 minutes until set. Let cool on pan for 2 minutes.
Remove to a cooling rack.

Used for Mummified Gingers, page 37.

# Oatmeal Cookies

## You'll Need

½ C. butter, softened

½ C. sugar

½ C. brown sugar

1 egg

½ tsp. vanilla extract

1 C. flour

½ tsp. baking soda

½ tsp. salt

¾ tsp. ground cinnamon

1½ C. quick-cooking rolled oats

## Directions

In a medium mixing bowl, beat butter, sugar and brown sugar on medium speed until blended. Beat in egg; stir in vanilla. In a small bowl, stir together flour, baking soda, salt and cinnamon; add to butter mixture, blending until incorporated. Stir in oats until blended. Shape dough and bake according to project directions.

Used for Oatmeal Bears, page 3.

# Marshmallow Fondant

## You'll Need

Vegetable shortening

1 (16 oz.) pkg. mini marshmallows

1 tsp. clear vanilla extract

1 (2 lb.) pkg. powdered sugar, sifted, divided

Paste food coloring as instructed in project

## Directions

Grease a large microwave-safe bowl with vegetable shortening and add marshmallows. Microwave on high for 1 minute. Using a large spoon, stir in vanilla and 4 tablespoons warm water until marshmallows are melted and mixture is smooth. Slowly stir in 5 to 6 cups powdered sugar, 1 cup at a time, until a sticky dough forms. Rub your hands thoroughly with shortening and knead dough in bowl until it's easy to work with. Sprinkle some of the remaining powdered sugar on work surface and knead dough until smooth and no longer sticky. (This is messy.) Divide dough into several balls and wrap each in plastic wrap. Unwrap one ball and make a well in the center. Add food coloring in well and knead dough around food coloring, gradually kneading the color through the ball to achieve desired color. Rewrap ball in plastic wrap. Repeat with remaining balls (keep one uncolored, if desired).

# Tips

You can wear plastic kitchen gloves to knead dough, if desired. However, it's much easier (and more fun) to use your hands. Keep dough well wrapped in plastic wrap whenever you're not working with it to keep it from drying out.

# Notes

What else can you do with fondant? Use it like edible clay to design animals, bugs or just about anything you can imagine. Or roll it out and cut to fit the tops of cupcakes and cookies for a smooth finish in place of frosting.

Used for Just Another Face in the Crowd, pages 14 to 16 and Barnyard Parade, pages 38 to 40.

# Marzipan

## You'll Need

1 (8 oz.) can almond paste

2 C. powdered sugar, divided

¼ C. light corn syrup

Paste food coloring as
instructed in project

## Directions

In a medium bowl, crumble almond paste and add 1 cup
powdered sugar. Using your hands, work powdered sugar
into almond paste until incorporated. Add ¾ cup powdered
sugar, continuing to work it with your hands. Add syrup
and work together until well blended. Sprinkle work surface
with remaining ¼ cup powdered sugar. Knead dough until
smooth and uniform. If dough is sticky, knead in a little more
powdered sugar. Wrap dough in plastic wrap and refrigerate
for 1 hour. Knead food coloring into small pieces of marzipan
until desired color is reached. To create a marbled effect,
work a small amount of two or three dough colors together
to reach desired amount of marbling. Keep unused marzipan
wrapped in plastic wrap.

# Tip

Keep dough well wrapped in plastic wrap whenever you're not working with it to keep it from drying out. Store leftover marzipan in refrigerator.

# Notes

Like fondant, marzipan is an edible clay-type substance molded to resemble mini fruits and veggies, flowers, leaves or any other number of items. It can be used to adorn cakes and cookies or can be eaten as candy.

Used for Sugar Wafer Garden Boxes, pages 20 and 21.

# Index

## Projects

## Recipes